Everything but the Kitchen Sink

Weird Stuff You Didn't Know About Food

By Frieda Wishinsky
and Elizabeth MacLeod
Illustrated by Travis King

■SCHOLASTIC

Thanks to Dr. Bill Wishinsky for his insightful
suggestions and for "being there" with love and support.
Thanks to David Wishinsky for his research
and for listening. Many thanks to Paul Wilson for his
help, ideas, and support always. We're grateful to
Brenda for her enthusiasm, openness to new ideas,
and her steadfast support. Thanks also to Travis for
adding a wonderful funky look to our words!

Text copyright © 2008 by Frieda Wishinsky and Elizabeth MacLeod
Illustration copyright © 2008 by Scholastic Inc.

ISBN 13: 978-0-545-00398-8
ISBN 10: 0-545-00398-9

10 9 8 7 6 5 4 3 2 1   08 09 10 11 12

Printed in the U. S. A.   23
First printing, January 2008
Illustrated by Travis King
Book design by Edward Miller & Kay Petronio

Contents

Introduction

Liz: Look at the variety of food on this menu! There are foods from all over the world. I think I'll have haggis.

Frieda: *What's haggis?*

Liz: A Scottish food that's cooked in a sheep's stomach. You should try some.

Frieda (gulping): *No, thank you.*

Liz: It's really good, sort of like a delicious meat loaf. What are you going to have?

Frieda: *I thought I'd order the tongue on rye sandwich with a pickle on the side. Want a taste?*

Liz (gulping): No, thank you.

Frieda: *It's strange. You like haggis because you've tasted it. But I haven't, and the idea of something cooked in a sheep's stomach turns my stomach. I like tongue because I've eaten it but . . .*

Liz: . . . the thought of eating a cow's tongue makes me queasy.

Frieda (laughing): *So what other weird foods have you eaten beside haggis?*

Liz: Hmmm . . . probably the weirdest is dulse, the seaweed snack that's eaten on the East and West coasts. How about you?

Frieda: *P'tcha—jellied calves feet. My mother insisted I try it when I was a kid. She said it was a great* delicacy in Poland, where she grew up. I thought it was the grossest food I've ever tasted.

Liz: It sure sounds gross! What are your favorite foods?

Frieda: That's easy. Anything with chocolate, like those amazing chocolate chip cookies you bake.

Liz: I love chocolate chip cookies, too. In fact, I think cookies are my favorite food!

Frieda: You know, we both love eating food and talking about it.

Liz: And we're both writers. Are you thinking what I'm thinking?

Frieda: Yeah! Let's write a food book. We could use books, encyclopedias, newspapers, magazines, and the Internet to find the most amazing facts. We'll write about weird foods and stories about the history of food. . . .

Liz: . . . and activities you can do with food and food records and. . . .

Frieda and Liz: Let's do it!

So we did and here it is!

Enjoy!

Frieda & Liz

Chapter One

Who Ate That?
Food Through the Ages

Food! We stare at it, sniff it, chew it, gulp it, dream about it, grow it, buy it, cook it, and bake it. Day after day, year after year, century after century, food has been and will always be an important part of our lives. Without it, we could not live.

Let's take a trip through the history of food to see what people ate long ago and what we eat today.

Bits and Bites

How do we know so much about food in ancient cultures like Egypt? Most of our knowledge comes from the graves of the rich and famous. The Egyptians and people of other ancient civilizations believed that the dead required all the provisions they had while they were alive, including food and drink, to help them on their way to the afterworld.

Of course, if you were a wealthy Egyptian, you had more stuff when you were alive and therefore more to take to the afterworld. And if you were a pharaoh, like King Tutankhamen (1370–1352 BCE), your grave was loaded with goodies.

What's So Good About a Flood? Ask the Ancient Egyptians.

• As far back as three thousand years ago, the ancient Egyptians loved floods—at least Nile River floods. When the Nile overflowed, it fertilized the land. They could grow grain and make their favorite foods, like pizza. Pizza? Egyptian food? Well, not the pizza we know today, but something similar—a flat bread with toppings.

And what did the Egyptians gulp down with their food? Beer! Some people think that the real reason they started to grow grain was to make beer.

7

When in Rome, Eat Fish.

• The ancient Romans loved fish. Fish became so fashionable in Rome two thousand years ago that some wealthy Romans kept tame ones in saltwater ponds. They also bought the biggest fish they could find at rowdy fish auctions. When they threw a banquet, the fish would be weighed on the table right in front of the guest. Talk about showing off!

Rome also had a bunch of emperors who were both loony and fish-lovers. Emperor Elagabalus (also known as Heliogabalus) who lived in the third century CE, served fish in a blue sauce so it would look like it was still swimming in the sea.

One fish Romans adored eating was a cross between an eel and a lamprey. Some Romans loved this fish so much that they kept it as a pet. One Roman lady decorated hers with gold earrings, while another wealthy Roman wept bitterly when his beloved fish died. He even built a monument to its memory. Now that's really loving your food!

Bits and Bites

Imagine if you were paid in salt to wash the dishes or take out the garbage? Salt has been so precious to humans since ancient times that part of a Roman soldier's salary was paid in salt. (And that's how we get the word *salary*.) It's been key in preventing food from spoiling.

China—Rice *is* Nice But . . .

• People have been eating rice in China since 5000 BCE, but only in southern China. Rice doesn't grow in the north, a much drier and colder region. Instead the northern Chinese grew grains such as millet, which they boiled into a kind of porridge.

• Although not everyone in China ate rice long ago, almost everyone drank tea. The Chinese have been sipping since 3000 BCE, and they haven't stopped yet.

• Why is Chinese food often cut into bite-size pieces before cooking? Is this a strange custom? No, it's a sensible solution to a cooking dilemma. China has few forests, so wood is scarce and expensive. By chopping food into small pieces, it cooks faster and uses less fuel.

Bits and Bites

The ancient Chinese loved throwing big banquets, often with as many as thirty-two courses. If you attended one of their banquets, you'd need lots of time and a large stomach to taste so many different dishes. But only the highest-ranking Chinese had to worry about consuming that much food. The higher your rank, the more courses you were served.

Munching During Europe's Dark Ages

• Times were tough for the poor in the Dark Ages, also known as the Early Middle Ages (around 450 CE to 1000 CE). The poor had difficulty growing enough food to feed their families. In bad crop years, many people starved. No matter how hard a poor farmer worked, it was almost impossible to move up in the world. The poor stayed poor and the rich stayed rich.

So what did the rich and poor eat in those times? The wealthy consumed lots of meat and bread and scoffed at vegetables and fruits. The rich thought vegetables were only fit for the poor. As for the poor, they ate a little meat, soup, and bread and whatever they could grow, including vegetables.

For most people, life was a bit easier in the later Middle Ages (about 1000 CE until the mid-1500s). It was a time of greater political stability, discoveries, inventions, and sumptuous feasts. Even the poor were invited to feasts, although there were strict rules about where people sat at a banquet and how they ate. The wealthy, of course, got the best seats and the best food.

Bits and Bites

How do you eat if you have only a few teeth left in your mouth? In the Middle Ages, that was the problem for many people who had poor diets, no fluoride, or dentists. Food in the Middle Ages was therefore often boiled, making it soft or mushy and easier to swallow.

Columbus Wasn't Looking for America. He Was Looking for Pepper.

• There's no question about it. Spices make food taste better and last longer. In the late 1500s, Europeans loved spices like pepper, cinnamon, nutmeg, and cloves. Unfortunately, spices had to be transported to Europe over slow, expensive, overland routes.

European kings and queens decided to send explorers to find faster, cheaper routes to the spice lands of India, China, and other parts of Asia. Explorers like Columbus and Magellan didn't sail off to conquer new lands but to fill their ships with spices and make buckets of money.

Although Columbus never discovered a quicker or more direct route to the Orient, he and his fellow explorers returned to Europe with tales of new lands and such exotic new foods as cocoa beans, chickpeas, wheat, and sugarcane.

Bits and Bites

What spice is called "king of the spices"? Paprika? Cinnamon? No! Pepper. It's one of the most used spices in the world and it doesn't only come in black. It comes in white, green, and pink also. They're all berries from the same plant—a vine that twines itself around trees and grows where it's steamy and hot, near the equator.

So what's the difference between the four peppers? Black pepper is the dried unripe berry. White pepper starts out like black, but is allowed to ripen longer. Green pepper is harvested before the fruit matures. As for pink, it's from the French island of Reunion and has a brittle, papery skin.

Dinner with George (Washington, That Is)

• Why did the first president of the United States, George Washington, and his wife, Martha, only dine alone two times in their twenty years of marriage? Did they hate being alone? No! It was simply good manners. In the mid-1700s in Virginia, good manners meant that if someone showed up on your doorstep in the evening, you invited your guest to stay for dinner.

What would you be served if you dropped in on the Washingtons of Mount Vernon? You'd be offered lots of wine and meat, such as pork, goose, and roast beef, along with a couple of vegetables like cabbage, corn, and potatoes. For dessert, you'd be treated to pies, tarts, cheese, apples, nuts and raisins, and more wine.

• For many Europeans who settled in the New World, what you ate depended upon where you came from and where you settled. The English brought apple pie to New England. The Dutch brought their coleslaw and cookies to New York, and the French introduced chowder, but used local fish.

Bits and Bites

Do you love corn? People in North America have adored this grass native to the Americas for centuries. We now know that corn's been around for thousands of years from the discovery of petrified cobs.

If not for corn, the Pilgrims might have starved those first cold winters in North America. Lucky for them, the Native Americans taught them how to plant corn by enriching the soil with small pieces of fish.

• Here are some other American dishes created as a mix of the Old World and the New: spoon bread (cornmeal, eggs, milk, and butter), cowpoke beans (beans and pork), mudbugs (crawfish), Haymaker's switchel (a drink made of apple vinegar, molasses, ginger, sugar, and water), and whaler's toddy (rum and sugar). The most popular colonial drinks were apple cider or rum, since no one trusted the safety of water.

Food from the Wild West: The Gold Rush—Tough Times—Bad Food

• In 1848, gold was discovered in California and people rushed out West hoping to get rich. A few people found gold but most only found hardship and unappetizing food.

Since most of the gold seekers were male, many had no idea how to cook, even if they could obtain the ingredients. Joseph R. Colin, who wrote about the eating habits of the western miners, said, "Some miners told of filling a pot with rice but no water, placing it on the fire and wondering why the result was not an edible fluffy piece."

Cowboy Chow

• Want some grub, chuck, or chow? Those are cowboy terms for food. A cowboy's diet consisted mainly of beef, beans, and potatoes.

It was hard for cowboys to get food on the range. That is, until Charlie Goodnight came up with a great idea. He loaded wagons with food supplies and created restaurants, called chuckwagons, that roamed along with the cowboys.

How would you like to eat "son-of-a-gun stew"—a cowboy dish made of beef parts cut up and stewed in greasy beef juice and flour gravy? Cow brains thickened the stew, and onions and chili added flavor. As Ramon F. Adams described this popular dish, "You throw everything in the pot but the hair, horns, and holler."

What Do You Eat Under Siege?

• How do you get through an attack on your city without starving? In the 1870s, the Parisians knew that the Prussians were about to lay siege to Paris so they filled storehouses with food. As the siege wore on, the supplies ran low. Soon people in Paris resorted to eating horses, donkeys, and mules. When they ran out of those poor beasts, they caught dogs, cats, and even rats and made stews and pies.

Then the day came when even that food ran out. Now what? Starve? Not the French! They realized that they had a zoo full of exotic animals that could become meals. That year, the French dined on elephants, zebras, and giraffes and survived the siege of Paris.

Bits and Bites

You did not go home hungry when you were invited to a wealthy Edwardian manor in England at the turn of the twentieth century. Dinner parties boosted a family's reputation and expensive foods, such as oysters, game, fancy pastries, fine chocolates, and champagne, filled the table. The dinners often ran to eight sumptuous courses.

War Foods: In the Trenches and at Home

• During World War I American soldiers complained bitterly about their food in the trenches. It was bad enough to face the enemy and sleep in cold, muddy conditions. But they had to eat what they called "goldfish" (a tasteless stew), canned salmon, and "monkey meat" (a strange-tasting French canned beef from Madagascar).

• During World War II, food was scarce everywhere. The folks at home had to contend with food rationing and "ration books," meatless meals, food substitutions, and making do with less.

Fifties Fare—When Fast Food Began to Take Off

• In 1945, World War II was over! Everyone was thrilled there was peace and overjoyed that there were no more ration books limiting food. Instead of fighting, people were busy building new lives, new homes, and new families. With all that activity, manufacturers invented and introduced convenience foods to cut down on the hours a housewife spent in the kitchen.

Most of all, the '50s were about fast and easy cooking. Here are some popular foods that filled the pantries and the tables of the '50s: Rice-A-Roni, Minute Rice, Sugar Pops, fish sticks, M&M's, and TV dinners.

Fad Today, Gone Tomorrow

• Food fads, like fashion fads, come and go like the wind. One day everyone's eating a fruit like kiwi. Then, almost overnight, kiwi goes out of style and other fruits like pomegranates and blackberries are suddenly all the rage. By the time you read this paragraph, a fruit, vegetable, or dish may be out of fashion and a new one anointed the latest and coolest food.

Plan a '50s Party

Invite your family and friends to a '50s party. Play '50s music (like the music from *Grease*), set the mood, and have a hula-hoop contest outdoors. Check out some favorite '50s foods and make a dish like tuna casserole, chicken á la king, or egg foo young.

Chapter Two

What's for Breakfast?

The word *breakfast* literally means to break your fast. Think about it—you've been fasting, or not eating, for about eight hours. After all that time without refueling, your energy is at a real low. That explains why some people wake up grumpy. It's also the reason why people who skip breakfast have trouble concentrating in the morning.

Scientists have shown that breakfast is good for the brain and makes you healthier, happier, and less stressed! Read on to find out more about the first—and most important meal—of the day.

Breakfast Facts

• When it comes to a breakfast drink, most kids choose orange juice. That's no surprise, but what else do people drink at breakfast? Would you believe that about an eighth of all the sodas sold in the United States are chugged down with breakfast—or instead of it?

• Can you guess what fruit is eaten most often first thing in the morning? Bananas. About 8 percent of breakfasts include them. This fruit has such breakfast *a-peel* that more than one third of all bananas eaten at home are munched on at breakfast.

• You may not think so, but you influence what your parents buy for breakfast. Almost all houses with kids in them buy ready-to-eat cereal. And if you eat that cereal, you're less likely to get a cold. You'll also fight a cold better than someone who doesn't eat cereal for breakfast.

Breakfast Through the Ages

• Orange juice is now the most popular drink at breakfast. However, long ago, especially in Europe, people chugged down beer first thing in the morning! Oranges were very rare treats there and the water and milk were often unsafe to drink. So beer or wine was the drink of choice. In England, the beer usually washed down a breakfast of bread and salted fish.

• In olden days, families didn't sit together at the kitchen table to have breakfast. They ate alone in their rooms. Today, people might do that too as they sit at their computer making last-minute changes to an assignment!

• Long ago, before electric lighting, people's days were organized around the hours when there was daylight. So people who ate breakfast might eat it very early, especially in the summertime when daybreak was around five A.M.

• You may think that ham and eggs are modern breakfast inventions, but they have a long history. Egyptians dug into this breakfast dish more than three thousand years ago.

• Have you ever heard the joke about the kid who ate a frog for breakfast? She figured the day could only get better. Ulysses S. Grant, president of the United States from 1869 to 1877, must have thought along the same lines: He started his day with a cucumber soaked in vinegar.

Other old-time American breakfasts are a little easier to choke down. In rural homes in the 1800s, fruit pies, especially apple, were often eaten for breakfast. People didn't top their pie with ice cream, though.

Bits and Bites

Some people in the northeastern United States used to eat radishes for breakfast. That vegetable is still popular for breakfast in Japan.

Egg-cellent Info

• It doesn't matter if you fry 'em, poach 'em, or scramble 'em, eggs are one of nature's most perfect foods. The only vitamin you won't find in them is vitamin C. Eggs are a great way to start the day. More than a third of all the eggs people eat are gulped down at breakfast.

eggs across America, and each year they produce approximately 5.5 billion dozen eggs.

The color of the eggshell doesn't tell you anything about the egg's taste, how good it is for you, or what color the hen's feathers are. But some people say that white eggs are laid by hens with whitish earlobes and brown eggs come from hens with red earlobes.

Most of those eggs are hen's eggs. Those are hard-working birds. There are about 240 million hens laying

Bits and Bites

That stringy white bit you see when you crack open an egg isn't a sign that the egg is bad. Those strands of egg white are called chalazae (ka-LAY-zee) and they keep the egg's yolk centered in the white.

Omelet in a Bag

A great way to start the day with a group of friends. And the cleanup is super simple.

WHAT YOU'LL NEED:

- An adult who can boil water
- A large pot of water
- 1-quart size Ziploc freezer bag per person
- A permanent marker
- 2 eggs per person
- Add-ins, such as grated cheese, chopped ham, and sliced peppers
- Tongs

1. With the adult's help, boil the water.

2. Have each friend write his or her name on a freezer bag.

3. Crack two eggs into each bag and zip it closed. Squish and shake the eggs until they're well combined.

4. Let each kid place in his or her bag whatever add-ins he or she likes. Then zip up each bag and shake it.

5. Carefully remove as much air as possible from each bag.

6. When the water is boiling, have an adult place each bag in the pot. Cook the omelets for thirteen minutes.

7. Using the tongs, have an adult remove each bag from the pot, and carefully open it. Slide each omelet onto a plate and dig in! (If an omelet isn't cooked, carefully re-seal its bag and boil it again for one or two more minutes.)

WHAT'S GOING ON?

Eggs are good for you because they're crammed with protein. It's packed into eggs in long, folded-up chains, or molecules, too small for you to see. As your omelet cooks, those molecules unfold. But when they bump into other protein molecules, they stick together. The hotter your omelet gets, the more the proteins stick. Your omelet turns solid and soon it's ready to eat.

Pour a Big Bowl

• No doubt about it, kids are cereal eaters. You'll eat about 15 pounds (6.8 kilograms) of cereal over the next year. Homes where children live munch about forty-seven boxes of cereal in a year, while kidless homes gobble only twenty-eight boxes of cereal. How many kinds of cereals are in your kitchen cupboard right now? Most homes have four.

The first breakfast cereal made in the United States was Granula. This tasty whole-grain flour dough was baked into dry leaves, broken into chunks and rebaked, then mashed into smaller chunks. Sound good? Even better, Granula was so hard that it had to be soaked overnight so it wouldn't crack your teeth. Strangely enough, the cereal didn't last long.

Experts think that people have been making cereal for 23,000 years. That's a lot of cereal! The word comes from Cerealia, which was the name of the ancient Roman ceremonies that honored the goddess Ceres. She was the goddess of grain, and that's what cereal is made of.

Thirteen years later, in 1876, Dr. John Harvey Kellogg created a breakfast cereal that he also called Granula. A lawsuit forced him to change the name to Granola. Kellogg seemed destined to be a cereal inventor. In 1894, he and his brother, Will Keith Kellogg, left some cooked wheat sitting around. They later found the wheat was stale but were too cheap to throw it out. So the brothers forced the mixture through large rollers, thinking the dough would come out in long sheets. Instead, it broke off into small flakes. The brothers decided to toast these, and the cereal was a hit.

The Kelloggs experimented with other grains, eventually creating corn flakes and Rice Krispies. The brothers' company is still one of the biggest cereal makers in America.

Bits and Bites

Breakfast cereals are the third most popular items sold at grocery stores, after sodas and milk.

Breakfast Around the World

• Most people across the globe drink the same things for breakfast. They often start with a fruit juice—orange juice is the most popular. Sometime during breakfast they likely gulp down milk (hot or cold) or some substitute. And many people won't start their day without coffee, tea, or hot chocolate.

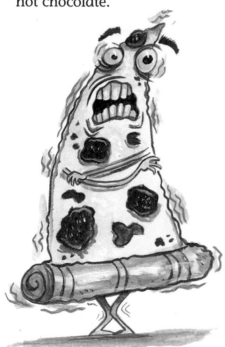

• When it comes to what people eat for breakfast, the choices are all over the map. In Thailand, Vietnam, and Cambodia, most people eat soup for breakfast. In the Philippines, look for garlic fried rice and pickles on the breakfast table. Farls are often on the menus of Northern Ireland—they're triangles of flat bread. If you're crazy for chocolate, then you'd love breakfast in Holland. The meal often includes bread topped with chocolate sprinkles or flakes. Don't forget many Americans' favorite breakfast—leftovers from the night before! Cold pizza, anyone?

Bits and Bites

In Korea, breakfast isn't a distinct meal with special dishes only eaten first thing in the morning. Breakfast foods aren't that different from those served at other meals of the day.

Breakfast Brainteaser

Use the clues below to match the country names to a breakfast often enjoyed there, then fill in your answers on the grid. One country has been written in to help you get started. The answers are on page 112.

COUNTRIES

- Australia
- England
- France
- India
- Italy
- Japan
- Mexico
- Middle East
- Poland
- Spain

ACROSS

1. huevos rancheros, tortillas, fruit
2. dosas, chapatis, coconut chutney
3. eggs, sausages, grilled tomatoes, toast, marmalade
4. café au lait, croissants
5. Vegemite on toast

DOWN

1. pita bread, olive oil, boiled eggs
2. chocolate con churros (hot chocolate with fritters)
3. cappuccino, biscotti
4. kielbasa sausage, sardines, sliced pickles
5. miso soup, rice with nori

Stacks O'Jacks

• If you're a pancake fan, then you'll be pleased to know that there's a special day for your favorite food. Pancake Tuesday takes place each year, forty-seven days before Easter. Whether you call these sweet flat treats griddle cakes, flapjacks, hot cakes, or whatever, it's a great day to celebrate.

• For more than five hundred years, women in Olney, England, have been celebrating Pancake Day with pancake races. Armed with a frying pan and a pancake, the women race to the finish line, madly flipping their flapjacks.

• Maybe you like your griddle cakes a little more straight edged? Then whip up a batch of waffles. Waffle irons made their appearance in Europe in the Middle Ages. Before Thomas Jefferson became president of the United States, he brought waffle irons from Europe to America.

• By the way, Americans celebrate National Waffle Day on August 24 each year to mark the anniversary of the first U.S. patent for the waffle iron. Get cooking!

• Some people top their pancakes or waffles with whipping cream, fruit, or jam. But for others, there's only one topping: maple syrup. It gets its name because it comes from the sap of maple trees.

To make maple syrup, workers first drive taps into the tree's phloem (the part that carries food throughout the tree). When the weather gives freezing nights and warm days, that change in temperature makes the sap move through the tree. As the sap flows past the tap, the sap drips into plastic tubes that eventually feed into a flat pan. There, the water is boiled out of the sap until you're left with maple syrup.

Bits and Bites

The record for pancake flipping is an amazing 349 flips in two minutes. The largest pancake anyone ever tossed measured a whopping 50 feet (15 meters) across.

Chapter Three

Why Don't Vampires Like Garlic?

Dogs walk under ladders. Rabbits hop on cracks. And what elephant would lumber around the jungle with a garland of garlic strung around its neck to ward off vampires? But humans can be a strange superstitious bunch, often about food. Every country and culture has its own food superstitions and traditions, while everyday food, such as salt and bread, are chock-full of dos and don'ts.

Good Luck, Bad Luck

All over Europe, people have linked good and bad luck with food.

• If your kettle boils slowly in Dorset, England, beware! According to some people, it might be bewitched. It could even contain a toad.

• Watch how you store your bread in Scotland. Long ago, an English soldier used an upside-down loaf of bread to signal a sneak attack on Scotland. From then on, people believed that if you stored unsliced bread with the rounded side down, someone would have trouble at sea or die.

• Have you ever noticed that a lettuce leaf looks like a lung? Unless you're a doctor, probably not. But because of the resemblance, an old English superstition suggests that eating lettuce can help cure lung disease.

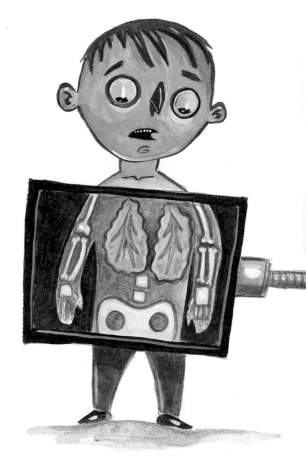

• Remember that jack-o'-lantern you carved out of a pumpkin last Halloween? The origin of that tradition goes back to an old Irish tale about a trickster named Jack who, at his death, was condemned to wander the earth. The light in the pumpkin was meant to brighten the way for travelers so they wouldn't be fooled by ghosts who appeared on All Hallows' Eve (another name for Halloween).

• When serving dinner, the Greeks never hand someone a knife. You might have an overpowering urge to fight your server.

• And don't garnish a plate with parsley. Parsley was considered sacred and suitable only for tombs, not plates.

Beware of Chopsticks

• If you visit Asia, never leave your chopsticks sticking up in food, especially not in rice. The Japanese stick chopsticks into rice only at funerals. Then they place the rice on the altar. Don't pass food from chopstick to chopstick. That's only done with the bones of a cremated body at a funeral.

• Never lie down after eating. Why? Is it bad for digestion? No. Some people in Japan think you'll turn into a cow.

• In China, never turn over a fish. If you do, a fishing boat might capsize. Want more good luck? The Chinese suggest you eat oranges or tangerines. And if a baby is born, boil eggs and dye them red. (Red is a lucky color.) Want long life? Eat long noodles.

• In Thailand, there is a long list of food don'ts. Here are a few: Don't eat before your elders, or you'll return as a dog in your next life. Don't eat other people's food without permission, or your throat will swell up. Don't eat chicken feet; they will give you bad handwriting. Don't eat turtles because you'll start to walk slowly. And don't eat dog, or the dog's spirit will possess you.

• If you're naughty in Vietnam, eat lots of rice. There's a sacred connection between the rice eater and the rice maker, so parents won't punish their children while they're eating rice.

The Americas and Corn—Superstitions or Just Good Ideas?

• Who are the "three sisters" according to an Iroquois myth? Three girls who hang around together? No. The Iroquois, who lived in eastern North America, believed they were corn, beans, and squash, three crops that were always grown and eaten together. The corn grew tall, the beans climbed the corn, and the squash trailed around and kept

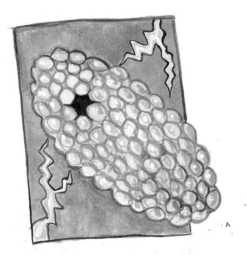

• The coastal Native American custom of planting a fish in every hill was another great idea. Fish was a great fertilizer and kept the corn growing.

• Corn was such an important crop that everything about it was considered precious. If a kernel was wasted, Native Americans believed God would become angry.

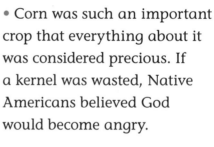

the weeds down. Eaten together, these three foods provided a well-balanced diet.

Have a Happy New Year or Else!

• New Year's and good luck go hand in hand. There are many New Year's superstitions around the world.

• If you've ever walked into a German specialty food store, particularly around New Year's, you'll see lots of beautiful marzipan animals, but especially pigs. In Germany, pigs are good luck.

• In some countries, little beans are baked in cakes on New Year's and Twelfth Night (January 5, which is twelve nights after Christmas). When the cakes are sliced, the person who finds the bean is lucky (especially if he or she doesn't choke on the bean or break a tooth).

In France some people stick little porcelain figurines in the cake for good luck.

• In Greece on New Year's Day, a special round sponge cake called *basilopita* (named after St. Basil) is served with coins hidden inside. If you are named Basil after the saint, you have to bake the cake.

• If you visit a Chinese family on New Year's, you might want to bring a gift, such as oranges. But never bring four oranges. The word for *four* in Chinese sounds like *death* and is unlucky. Fish is a good bet on the Chinese New Year, since the word *fish* in Chinese sounds like luck.

Lucky Food Match-Up

There are many countries that have lucky New Year's foods. Can you guess which of these foods are considered lucky in the following countries? The answers are on page 112.

Foods	Countries
boiled cod	Cambodia
pancakes	Italy
lentils	Hungary
doughnuts	Denmark
roast pig	Holland
sticky rice cakes with sweet beans	France

Birthdays, Wishes, and Toasts

• What's your favorite kind of birthday cake? Chocolate? Vanilla with strawberry icing? How about a round cake made with cereal, moistened with water, sweetened with honey, and turned over on a griddle? That's the kind of birthday cake the Romans would serve when someone reached his or her fiftieth birthday. (And in those days, fifty was considered pretty old.) It wasn't till the sixteenth century that cakes with eggs and sugar were baked.

• Why do we put candles on a cake and light them? The custom evolved because light from fire has long been connected to celebrations. As for the tradition of blowing out the candles and making a wish, some people say that's because blowing out a candle is symbolic of blowing away the past. Once you blow away the past, you can wish for the future.

• If you've attended a wedding, you may have heard a toast to the bride and groom. The tradition may have started in Greece. The Greeks would hold a cup of wine in one hand, look up to the sky, and pray with both arms raised, imagining they were sharing their wine with the gods. Then they'd drink the wine and hope the gods would think well of them.

But why the word *toast*? That's because the Romans used to soak a piece of burned bread in their wine, probably to remove undesirable flavors from it. Romans would say, "Let's drink a toast," and mean the glass with the toast floating in it.

Keep the World Going— Dye an Egg

• Why is Easter all about eggs and bunnies? Eggs have long been symbols of the beginning of the universe. A Latin proverb reads, "All life comes from the egg," and Easter is celebrated in spring, a time of rebirth and renewal.

• The bunny, especially the hare, goes way back as a symbol of fertility. Rabbits have large families and symbolize new life. The legend of the Easter bunny started in Germany. Children were told that the Easter bunny left them colored eggs, but only if they were good.

• Eggs were dyed and eaten in ancient Egypt, Persia, Greece, and Rome. They were given as gifts to celebrate the coming of spring. In many cultures, red eggs were the most popular. Red has long been considered a magic color. Witches wore red petticoats, and some types of red berries were thought to ward off evil.

Scary Tales About Salt and Garlic

• Salt has been so sought after that many cultures have superstitions and stories about it. If someone said you were "worth your salt," you were important.

• Some people believe that you should bring salt to a person who's just moved into a new home, for good luck. But don't drop the salt or you'll have bad luck. If you do drop it, grab some salt quickly and throw it over your shoulder. Then you'll cancel out the bad luck.

• Why is garlic hated, feared, and loved? Centuries ago, people thought it was so magical that they worshipped it. They thought garlic could cure disease, help aches and pains, and give people courage. As for vampires, they're not keen on strong odors either, so you can guess why garlic would keep them away.

Chapter Four

Don't Grunt.
It's a Piece of Cake.

Food is everywhere. We talk about it. We think about it. We party with it, plan it, worry about it, and work for it. We talk about food even when we're not thinking about producing, buying, or eating it. English is full of strange food expressions and names, and each one's path into common usage is different. Sometimes it's startling, sometimes it's funny, and sometimes it's just plain weird.

Let's Talk Fruit

• The term *forbidden fruit* was first written in the Bible in the story of Adam and Eve who were warned not to eat what many people think was an apple in the Garden of Eden. Swayed by a smooth-talking snake, Adam and Eve didn't listen to God and tasted the forbidden fruit. Soon Adam and Eve were kicked out of the Garden of Eden. The term *forbidden fruit* was popularized in the seventeenth century to mean something you're supposed to stay far away from—and not just apples.

• Why is New York City called The Big Apple? It's not shaped like an apple and there aren't a lot of apples growing there. The expression became popular when jazz musicians in the 1930s boasted about playing in The Big Apple— New York City. If you did, that meant you'd made it big. In 1971, New York City's convention bureau started using the term to attract visitors.

Two Relaxed Vegetables

• If you're as "cool as a cucumber," you're pretty relaxed. But what's serene about a skinny, green vegetable with seeds? John Gay first used the expression in 1732 in a book. Back then it was believed that cucumbers were cool to the touch even on warm days. And in 1970, cucumber coolness was scientifically proven. We now know that since a cucumber is full of water, it's 20°F (11.1°C) cooler than the temperature of the air.

Bits and Bites

Do you love mashed potatoes, French fries, or baked potatoes? You're not alone. Many people today consider the potato the most important vegetable in the world. From its current popularity, you'd think it's been eaten worldwide for centuries. Not so. Only a few people like the Andes Indians from the mountainous regions of South America have cultivated potatoes for centuries. They were even the first to dehydrate potatoes by spreading them out to dry in the sun.

• Do you sit around all day and watch television? Then you might be called a couch potato. You can thank Tom Lacino of Pasadena, California, for that expression. Lacino, a member of a group that humorously opposed the exercise and dieting fads of the 1970s, made up the term on July 15, 1976,

in a telephone conversation. He said his life focused on the "Boob Tube," a name for TV. And since *tubers* is another name for potatoes, Lacino coined the term *couch potato.*

In Trouble with Pastry

• English is loaded with cake and pie expressions. Queen Marie Antoinette of France was accused of saying, "Let them eat cake," when she heard that the poor were starving in France. That accusation added to her already shaky reputation and may have led to her death. The French guillotined her during the Revolution in 1793. Marie Antoinette probably never said those famous words, but the phrase stuck to her like molasses. Rousseau, a famous French writer, first wrote those words in his book *Confessions*, three years before it was attributed to Marie Antoinette.

• The expression *cakewalk* probably started in the United States in pre–Civil War days when slaves held competitions to see which couple could walk with the greatest style and elegance. The winners won a cake and their graceful walk became known as a *cakewalk*. In the 1870s, the term *cakewalk* was also used when a boxer had an easy victory over his opponent. By the 1940s, *cakewalk* evolved into the expression "It's a piece of cake," meaning something is as easy to accomplish as baking a cake.

• Have you ever seen "a pie in the sky?" Probably not, and the expression means just that, something impossible. It originated in 1910 when a trade union song, "The Preacher and the Slave," mockingly suggested that although things are tough for you now, one day you'd be rewarded in heaven with a scrumptious slice of pie.

A Little Piggy Said

• What's so fascinating about pigs? In the Jewish and Muslim religions, even a nibble of pig meat is forbidden. But many people around the world enjoy eating pork, ham, and bacon (just to name a few pig products), and English is full of pig-linked expressions.

• The expression *piggybank* has nothing to do with pigs but snuck into our language by mistake. During the Middle Ages, dishes and pots were made of an economical ceramic called pygg. Housewives would drop a coin in their pygg to save money. Along the way, the term *pygg* got mixed up with the word *pig*, and the piggybank was born.

• Have you ever watched an actor "ham it up?" Ham actors are show-offs, but what does that have to do with pigs? The connection may be that ham fat was used to remove makeup in the nineteenth-century theaters, or perhaps it came from a minstrel show called *The Hamfat Man*, about a bad actor. A third possibility is that the word *ham* is a play on the word *amateur*.

• You probably thought that pigs couldn't fly, so of course the saying "when pigs fly" means something that could never happen. Well in 1909, a pig did fly, although not with its own wings. An early aviator, Lord Brabazon, took one up in a basket tied to the wing of his plane to prove that pigs could fly. To everyone's relief, both the pig and Lord Brabazon landed safely on the ground.

Why Is It Called That?

Grunt

Can dessert grunt? Ask a Canadian and you'll learn that if you make a special pudding, you'll hear a grunting sound while it's being steamed. This tasty dish is often made with blueberries, raspberries, huckleberries, or even rhubarb and is served with thick cream. So remember, if you want your dessert to not only taste good but talk to you, make a grunt!

Mudbugs

If you live in Louisiana in the southern United States, you might be invited to feast on mudbugs. Before you say no, consider this. Mudbugs are not real bugs like cockroaches or earwigs. They're crawfish, small crustaceans, or shellfish, somewhat like lobster.

Despite their name, mudbugs make a tasty dish, especially boiled quickly in a pot with corn, garlic, potatoes, and sausage and smothered in spices.

Slugburgers

Unlike its name, this burger, which originated in Corinth, Mississippi, doesn't have a drop of slug in it. It's made of beef and bread or soybean meal and deep fried. So why the weird name? There are lots of theories. A slug used to be the name for a nickel, and long ago, that's all this beef dish cost. Some think that if you ate too many of these burgers, you'd feel like you'd been slugged in the stomach. But perhaps the best explanation of all is when the meat patty was served cold after being fried in lard, it resembled, you guessed it—a slippery, slimy slug.

Hush Puppy

If you live in the southern United States, you can feast on a hush puppy. No, you wouldn't eat a dog but a finger-shaped croquette-like dumpling made of cornmeal and deep fried.

Why is it named after a noisy dog? Here are three possible reasons. When an African cook in Atlanta fired up some catfish-and-cornmeal dumplings, a puppy nearby began to bark. "Hush, puppy," said the chef, as he tossed it a plateful of dumplings. Another story says that when the dogs of hunters and trappers were hungry, a dish of cornmeal cooked on the campfire would calm them down. And the third story has *hush puppy* originating in the Civil War, with Confederate soldiers. When the soldiers saw the Yankees approaching, they tossed food at their dogs and begged them to hush.

What's in a Name?

• Remember these famous nursery rhyme words: "Four-and-twenty blackbirds baked in a pie"? Well, that actually happened at banquets in the Middle Ages. Birds were baked under a piecrust but just enough to stun them. When the pie was cut, the birds flew out to the amusement of the onlookers. Sometimes not just birds popped out of pies—but rabbits, frogs, turtles, and even dwarfs.

• You might think Baked Alaska is a pie baked in the shape of the state. But it's a dessert made of ice cream in hot pastry and topped with meringue (whipped egg whites and sugar). Many people take credit for this unusual treat, including a physicist named Benjamin

Thompson, who also invented the coffee percolator. In 1867, Chef Charles Ranhofer at Delmonico's Restaurant in New York City claimed he came up with the idea to celebrate the purchase of Alaska by the United States from Russia.

Star-Crossed Food

• In the late 1800s, Helen Porter had a remarkable voice and sang opera around the world, changing her name to Nellie Melba (after her home city of Melbourne). Famous chef Auguste Escoffier was so impressed with her glorious voice

that he named two dishes in her honor, a delightful peach dessert called peach Melba and a twice-grilled dry cracker called Melba toast. Which one do you think Nellie liked best?

The light and airy meringue-based fruit-and-whipped-cream dessert Pavlova is adored in Australia and New Zealand. So was the famous Russian prima ballerina Anna Pavlova (1882–1931), who toured those two countries and inspired the pie. Chefs from both Australia and New Zealand claim to have originated the dessert in her honor.

Famous Food from North to South

• Any New Yorker growing up in the 1940s or 1950s will remember egg creams. This fizzy soda fountain drink contains neither eggs nor cream and was invented around the turn of the century when eggs were expensive. So why is it called an egg cream, without either ingredient? Its foamy top and rich flavor suggests eggs and cream, but it's made of whole milk, bottled seltzer, and chocolate syrup.

In 1899, Jules Alcatiore took over his family's restaurant, Antoine's, in New Orleans, Louisiana. Alcatiore became a pioneer in cooking oysters. When he created an oyster dish made of raw spinach, parsley, chopped green onion tops, hot pepper, salt, breadcrumbs, butter, and oysters, a customer was said to have raved, "Why, this is as rich as Rockefeller." And so the dish, oysters Rockefeller, named after one of the richest families in America, was created.

Food Fight!

• Caesar Cardini, not Emperor Julius Caesar, invented the Caesar salad. Cardini's salad was a combination of Romaine lettuce, garlic, croutons, grated Parmesan, coddled eggs, and Worcestershire sauce. On July 4, 1924, Cardini's daughter Rosa claims she watched her father toss the salad for the first time in Tijuana, Mexico. Livio Santini, an elderly resident of Tijuana, says he made the salad in 1925 from his mother's recipe when he was eighteen. He accused Caesar Cardini of stealing his recipe.

Guess how these popular food expressions and food names came to be.

1. The expression "chew the fat," which means to have a casual conversation about anything, comes from:

    a. the Inuit people who chewed on whale like chewing gum.

    b. a man stranded on a desert island who chewed the fat on his last chunk of meat for a week before he was rescued.

2. The expression "happy as a clam," meaning you're satisfied with life, comes from:

    a. a man who opened a clam one day and thought it was smiling.

    b. the fact that clams can be caught only at low tide, so if it's high tide, the clams are safe—and happy.

3. The phrase to "egg someone on," which means encourage someone to do something he or she shouldn't, originated with:

    a. a boy in nineteenth-century America who was encouraged by his friends to toss rotten eggs at his teacher.

    b. an Old English word, **eggian**, meaning to incite, spur on, or encourage.

4. Thousand Island dressing was introduced by:

    a. a sailor who visited a thousand islands and put some of the ingredients from each in his dressing.

    b. George Boldt, one-time owner of the Waldorf Astoria hotel in New York, who named the dressing to honor the thousand islands on the St. Lawrence River, the beautiful area where it was first prepared.

The answers are on page 112.

Chapter Five

Snack Attack!

There are so many delicious ways to snack and ruin your appetite. Whether you like your snacks sweet or sour, cold or hot, crunchy or chewy, you'll find them all in the next few pages.

The world's favorite snack is also the world's oldest snack: popcorn. Native Americans have been eating it for thousands of years. Today, Americans gobble up more than one billion pounds of popcorn every year. That works out to about 70 quarts (66 liters) per person. Unlike most snacks, popcorn is good for you—as long as you leave off the butter and salt.

The Hard Facts About Soft Drinks

• Soda or pop? Depending on where you live in the United States, soft drinks are known as one or the other. No matter what you call them, they make up more than 25 percent of all the drinks chugged down in America. Every year, Americans drink more than 15 billion gallons (60 billion liters)!

• How were sodas invented? For hundreds of years, people had been taking baths in fizzy water or mineral water. Eventually someone got the idea that if it was good for the outside of your body, then maybe it was good for the inside, too. It wasn't long before people began adding sugar and flavoring—and soft drinks were born.

Nice Slice

• If you're like most kids, then pizza is one of your favorite foods. Pepperoni is the number one topping in the United States—while anchovies are in last place.

• About one thousand years ago in Naples, Italy, circles of baked dough covered with herbs became popular. Tomatoes weren't added until the late 1600s.

• Pizzas are now eaten in almost every country, and each nation has its favorite toppings. In Japan, eel and squid are tops, while Costa Ricans prefer coconut. Brazilians put green peas on pizza, and chocolate and fruit are also favorite toppings there. In Hong Kong, your pizza may come with Thousand Island salad dressing instead of tomato sauce. The combination of ham and pineapple is known as "Hawaiian" and is a big hit in the western United States, Australia, and Canada—but not Hawaii!

Hot Dogs

• Hot dogs, frankfurters, wieners, red hots, tube steaks—whatever you call them, Americans love them. Each year, every person in the United States eats on average sixty hot dogs.

Some people claim the hot dog was invented in the late 1600s by a German butcher named Johann Georghehner. The long, thin sausage reminded people of a dachshund, and it was served warm, so *hot dog* seemed like a good name.

Hot dogs are a type of sausage, and sausages have been around for thousands of years. Frankfurt, Germany, claims to have created a thick, soft pork sausage around 1484 and it was named "the frankfurter" for the city. In 1805, Vienna, Austria, became famous for a pork-and-beef sausage. Vienna is called Wien in German so you can guess where the name *wiener* started.

• No one knows for sure when hot dogs got wrapped in a bun. What's certain is that the snack was first sold at a baseball game in St. Louis, Missouri, in 1893, and they've been sold at ballparks ever since.

Bits and Bites

What do you put on your hot dog? America's favorite topping is mustard, but some people like mayonnaise, French fries, and canned corn. There are hotdoggers who say you must never add ketchup!

Chip, Chip, Hooray!

• It all started back in 1853 in Saratoga Springs, New York, with a bad-tempered chef and a picky diner. The customer sent his fried potatoes back to the restaurant's kitchen, saying they were too thick and soggy. Out went another order of fries and back they came again.

The chef, George Crum, was furious. He decided to show the diner who was boss. Crum sliced the potatoes as thinly as he could, then he salted them heavily to make them taste as bad as possible. But the customer gobbled down the dish and asked for more! Potato chips were created, although Crum originally called them potato crunches.

Potato chips were first stored in barrels or tins. But the chips at the bottom of the container became damp and stale. Now, chips are packaged in plastic bags. Just before the bags are sealed, nitrogen gas is blasted in to keep the chips fresh longer and to reduce crushing.

Snack on the Run

• Lightweight, high in energy, easy to store—trail mix and granola bars can be great snack foods when you're hiking or camping and can't carry fresh fruit or vegetables.

It's easy to make trail mix. Just combine your favorite dried fruits and nuts with seeds, cereal, and a few treats such as pretzels, mini marshmallows, or chocolate chips. Store in an airtight container.

• Take a delicious, healthy breakfast food, shape it into a bar, and you've got a terrific snack you can take just about anywhere. Granola bars start with rolled oats, nuts, honey, and sometimes a little dried fruit. This granola is shaped into a bar and baked—just a little to make a chewy bar or a bit longer until it's crisp. The fiber, vitamins, and minerals found in many granola bars can make this a great snack choice.

Cookie Jar

• Chewy or crispy, there's nothing like a handful of cookies with a big glass of milk for a delicious—and somewhat nutritious—snack. The word cookie comes from the Dutch word *koekje*, which means "little cake."

• One of the most famous cookies was invented in 1930 in Whitman, Massachusetts. Ruth Wakefield

Haystacks

Try making these easy, no-bake chocolate cookies.

WHAT YOU'LL NEED:

- $3/4$ cup chocolate chips, melted
- 2 tablespoons butter, melted
- 2 tablespoons milk
- 1 $3/4$ cups corn flakes
- $3/4$ cup sweetened, flaked coconut

1. In a large bowl, mix together chocolate, butter, and milk.

2. In a medium bowl, slightly crush corn flakes. Mix in coconut. Add to chocolate mixture and stir until coated.

3. Place spoonfuls of mixture on a baking sheet.

4. Refrigerate two hours, until firm. Makes about two dozen cookies.

was baking chocolate cookies but discovered she had no cocoa powder. So Ruth added small pieces of semisweet chocolate instead, figuring they'd melt during baking. But they didn't. Ruth named her invention the "chocolate crispie," but you probably call it the chocolate chip cookie.

The Hungry Captain

• The year was 1847 when sea captain Hanson Gregory found himself in the middle of a terrible storm. He needed both hands to hold the wheel of his ship, but he had a fried cake in one of them. What to do? Hanson speared the cake on one of the spokes of the wheel

and his snack stayed there until he had time to eat it.

Usually the center of these cakes was undercooked, but Hanson had poked out the soggy middle. He was delighted with his new invention. Soon everybody was punching the holes in their cakes before frying them, and the doughnut was invented.

It's a good story, but no one knows for sure if it's true. People also argue whether the snack should be spelled *donut* or *doughnut*. In different parts of the United States, they're also called twists, old-fashioneds, long johns, crullers, and more. Even doughnut holes are now popular.

You can glaze them, spread on icing, fill them with jam or cream, or add fruit or nuts—however they're prepared, Americans eat about ten million doughnuts every year. You don't have to be a cartoon character to say, "Mmmm, doughnuts."

When Money Grew on Trees

• Thousands of years ago, the Mayan people of Central America brewed a drink from the beans of the cacao tree and discovered how delicious cocoa could be. The Mayans called cacao the "food of the gods" and decorated their temples with pictures of cocoa pods.

When the Aztecs came along, they drank a form of hot chocolate. The word *chocolate* comes from the Aztec word *xocolatl*, which means bitter water.

It wasn't until 1847 that the world finally figured out how to *eat* chocolate, not just drink it. About thirty years after that, a Swiss company added milk to chocolate—the result was milk chocolate.

Today, chocolate is one of the most popular flavors and foods. People around the world spend more than $20 billion on chocolate every year. Over your lifetime, you'll probably eat about 353 pounds (160 kilograms).

Dandy Candy

• It's pretty simple. You take sugar, dissolve it in water, add a little flavoring and color, and, depending on how you cook it, you get gummi bears, mints, candy corn, jelly beans, or any of the other sweet treats known as candy. The word comes from the Arabic *qandi*, meaning "crystallized sugar."

• Gum is a favorite candy among most kids. The first bubble gum ever sold was called Blibber-Blubber. For some reason, people didn't like the way the bubbles burst into sticky pieces all over their faces, so it was never a success. When a candy maker created a batch of bubble gum that didn't pop and stick, he colored it pink because that was the only coloring he had around. That's why bubble gum is pink today.

• Another candy maker got tired of his chocolate treats melting in the summer. So he created a hard mint candy shaped like a circle with a hole in the middle. It looked like a tiny life preserver so he called his invention Life Savers.

• More than one hundred years ago, someone trying to make caramels made a mistake, and fudge was the delicious result. *Fudge* also means "to cheat or cover a mistake," so that's why this snack got its name.

Bits and Bites

Swallowing your gum isn't a great idea, but it won't really hurt you. It'll probably pass right through your body and out the other end looking much the same as it did when you swallowed it.

I Scream, You Scream . . .

• . . . we all scream for ice cream! This summertime snack probably originated in ancient Rome, when slaves had to go back and forth from snowy mountains carrying ice to freeze fruit drinks. In the 600s, a Chinese king had a recipe for combining ice and milk, and the treat spread from there. In the late 1700s, Americans became the first to call it "ice cream," although they originally named it "iced cream."

• Some people say the ice-cream cone was created in the late 1800s. Others say it was invented at the St. Louis World's Fair in 1904, when an ice-cream vendor ran out of cups. The baker in the next booth rolled up a wafflelike pastry, and the world had a new treat.

Bits and Bites

Did you know that pigs love ice cream—unless it's mint flavored!

It's Not Summer Without Them!

• Kids love them, so it's only right that a kid invented the Popsicle. Back in 1905, Frank Epperson of San Francisco was eleven years old. One winter night, he accidentally left a fruit drink with a stir stick in it out on the porch.

Temperatures plummeted that night. When Epperson retrieved his drink the next morning, it was frozen solid. He tasted it and showed it to his friends, but that was all. The world had to wait eighteen years before Epperson patented

his invention. He called it the Epsicle ice pop. Huh? Luckily, kids got involved again in the story. By now, Epperson was a father, and his children started calling his invention the Popsicle. Soon their dad (or "pop") called it that, too.

• Can you guess what the most popular Popsicle flavor is? Orange.

Bits and Bites

May 27 is National Grape Popsicle Day. Cherry Popsicle Day is August 26, and September 2 is the date for Blueberry Popsicle Day. Don't like Popsicles? Try celebrating National Creamsicle Day on August 14!

Chapter Six

There's a Lab in My Kitchen.

You may think you're cooking and baking in your kitchen, but you're really doing chemistry and physics experiments.

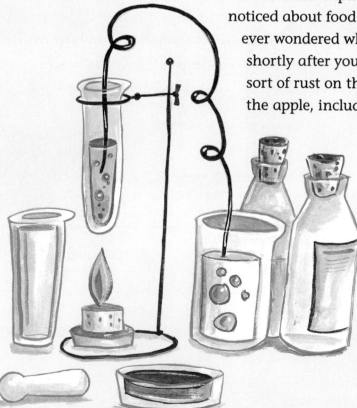

Science can explain a lot of things you've noticed about food. For example, have you ever wondered why an apple turns brown shortly after you cut it? It's forming a sort of rust on the surface. Substances in the apple, including one that contains iron, react with oxygen in the air.

Before you try any of these experiments and recipes, be sure to get permission from an adult. Let an adult help you with anything hot or sharp. And hey, clean up the kitchen when you're finished!

Soda Fountain

Make an incredible soda fountain, but be sure to do it outside!

WHAT YOU'LL NEED:

- An adult's permission to make a really big mess
- Mentos candies (or wintergreen Life Savers)
- Test tube or sheet of paper rolled into a narrow tube
- A two-liter bottle of diet cola
- Small piece of cardboard

1. Find a wide open place outside, or you'll be doing a lot of cleaning after.
2. Place twelve Mentos in the test tube or roll them into the tube of paper.
3. Open the bottle of soda and place the cardboard over the top.
4. Position the tube of candies over the mouth of the bottle so that all of them will drop in at the same time.
5. Whip the cardboard out from under the tube and run!

WHAT'S GOING ON?

Each candy has lots and lots of tiny pits all over its surface. Carbon dioxide gas in the cola—the gas is what gives the soda its fizz—forms bubbles at those pits. That releases the gas from the liquid, and the gas pushes the liquid out of the bottle and high into the sky!

No one knows why diet cola makes a higher fountain than regular cola. An added bonus is that the diet drink is less sticky to clean up.

Bits and Bites

When you open a can of soda, the *whoosh* you hear is the carbon dioxide rushing out of the can.

Wacky Cake

Discover a delicious reaction when baking soda and vinegar meet.

WHAT YOU'LL NEED:

- An adult's permission to use an oven
- 1 $1/2$ cups all-purpose flour
- 1 cup white sugar
- $1/4$ cup unsweetened cocoa powder
- 1 teaspoon baking soda
- 1 teaspoon vanilla
- 5 tablespoons vegetable oil or melted butter or margarine
- 1 tablespoon white vinegar
- 1 cup lukewarm water

1. Preheat the oven to 350°F (180°C).

2. Sift the flour, sugar, cocoa, and baking soda into an 8-inch (20-centimeter) cake pan that's lined with aluminum foil.

3. Make three holes in the mixture. Pour the vanilla into the first hole, the oil into the second hole, and the vinegar into the third one.

4. Quickly pour the water over the mixture and stir well. Be careful not to rip the foil.

5. Bake the cake for thirty minutes, until done. Cool for fifteen minutes in the pan on a cooling rack. Then turn the cake upside down onto the rack and remove from the pan and foil. Cool completely. If you like, frost your cake with your favorite icing or sift powdered sugar on top.

WHAT'S GOING ON?

As you mix the cake batter, you add air bubbles to it. When the baking soda meets the vinegar, carbon dioxide gas is produced. It causes the air bubbles to expand, which makes the cake rise. The flour in the batter strengthens the walls of the bubbles so they don't collapse when you take the cake out of the oven. The oven's heat also turns the water in the batter into steam and that adds lift.

Bits and Bites

The holes in Swiss cheese are caused by carbon dioxide released when bacteria in the cheese "burp." The holes are called eyes. Swiss cheese with no holes in it is referred to as being "blind."

Dancing Raisins

These wrinkly grapes really know how to bust a move.

WHAT YOU'LL NEED:

Colorless soda, such as club soda, 7UP, or Sprite

A tall, clear glass or plastic cup

Raisins

1. Pour the soda into the glass.

2. Drop six or seven raisins into the glass and watch what happens.

WHAT'S GOING ON?

As you found out on page 59, soda is full of carbon dioxide bubbles. When those bubbles cling to the raisins, they make the dried grapes more buoyant and the raisins bob to the soda's surface. There, the bubbles burst, making the raisin sink to the bottom again.

Don't have any soda around? Fill the glass halfway with water. Stir in 1 teaspoon (5 milliliters) of baking soda until it's completely dissolved. Add raisins to the glass, then slowly pour in white vinegar until the glass is about three-quarters full. Baking soda and vinegar give off bubbles of carbon dioxide when they combine.

If someone ate all of the raisins in your house, try using mothballs or pieces of uncooked pasta. What works best?

Chomp and Glow

Learn a long word to impress your friends and get fresh breath too.

WHAT YOU'LL NEED:

- A mirror
- Wint-O-Green Life Savers
- A very dark room

In front of the mirror, and with your mouth open, crunch down on a Life Saver.

WHAT'S GOING ON?

See those sparks? When you bite into the candy, your chompers split up sugar molecules. That makes an electric field, which excites nitrogen gas in the air. The nitrogen gives off ultraviolet radiation, which you can't see. But the UV makes the wintergreen flavoring in the candy give off a blue flash. Many hard candies flash when you crunch them but the flash is usually too faint for you to see. The flash is called triboluminescence. This name comes from two words that mean "light and rubbing."

Bits and Bites

Ever noticed how after you've had a mint or used mint toothpaste that a glass of water seems much colder? That's because mint not only affects your taste buds, it also triggers pain receptors in your mouth. The temperature and flavor of anything you taste next is exaggerated.

Tasty!

Are you a supertaster, a nontaster, or somewhere in between?

WHAT YOU'LL NEED:

- A cotton swab
- Green food coloring
- Reinforcement rings (for paper with holes punched in it)
- A mirror
- A magnifying glass

1. Using the cotton swab, dab some food coloring onto the tip of your tongue.

2. Stick a reinforcement on your tongue.

3. Looking in the mirror, use the magnifying glass to count the pinky bumps or dots inside the ring.

WHAT'S GOING ON?

The pink dots on your tongue are your *papillae*, tiny bumps that house your taste buds. If you've got lots of papillae, then you've got lots of taste buds and you're a supertaster.

No one knows for sure exactly how many papillae supertaster kids have. An adult supertaster would count at least twenty-five bumps in the circle. Scientists do know that half of all people have a regular sense of taste, one quarter are supertasters, and one quarter are nontasters, or people who have a less sensitive sense of taste.

Your eyes also affect your taste buds.

WHAT YOU'LL NEED:

- Clear lime soda
- Two tall glasses
- Green food coloring
- Small paper cups
- A friend to work with

1. Pour half of the soda into each glass.

2. Add food coloring to the soda in one of the glasses to make the soda pale green.

3. Pour soda from one glass into a paper cup. Pour soda from the other glass into another cup.

4. Ask your friend to taste the colorless soda. How quickly can he or she figure out the flavor? Then let him or her taste the colored soda. How quickly does he or she figure out this taste? Try this experiment with other friends and other flavors.

WHAT'S GOING ON?

Your eyes tell your taste buds what to expect. This is a survival technique. Often food that's gone bad changes color or looks different.

Bits and Bites

A chicken has forty-five taste buds, a dog has two thousand, and a catfish has one hundred thousand. How many do you have? About ten thousand.

Shake, Shake, Shake

The freshest butter you've ever tasted

WHAT YOU'LL NEED:

- A small jar with screw-on lid
- Whipping cream
- A marble, washed
- A friend with strong arms
- Bread

1. Fill the jar halfway with cream.

2. Drop in the marble and screw on the lid.

3. Shake the jar as hard as you can for as long as you can.

4. Pass the jar to your friend to shake.

5. Keep shaking the jar until you can't hear the marble clunking any more. That means your cream is now whipped cream.

6. Shake some more until you hear the marble again. Your butter is finally ready! Pour off the liquid and spread your butter on the bread.

WHAT'S GOING ON?

Cream has milk fat in it; that's what makes it creamy. The droplets of fat wear little protein coats to keep them dissolved in the milk and not clump together. But the shaking removes those coats, and the fat droplets stick together and form butter. The liquid you poured off is buttermilk.

You've just made unsalted butter. If you don't like the taste, try the experiment again, adding a pinch of salt to the cream before you start shaking.

Ice Cream in a Bag

Find out how science can help you make a cool treat.

WHAT YOU'LL NEED:

- $\frac{1}{2}$ cup half-and-half cream
- $\frac{1}{2}$ teaspoon vanilla
- 1 tablespoon white sugar
- 2 quart-size Ziploc freezer bags
- 1 gallon-size Ziploc freezer bag
- 4 cups crushed ice
- $\frac{1}{4}$ cup salt
- Gloves

1. Pour the cream, vanilla, and sugar into one of the quart-size bags. Seal the bag tightly after first pressing out as much air as possible. (This will help keep the bag from opening in the next steps.)

2. Place the bag inside the other quart-size bag. Press out the air and zip the second bag shut. (The double-bagging reduces the risk of leaks.)

3. Put the bags in the large bag. Fill the bag with ice and sprinkle it with the salt. Press out the air and seal the bag.

4. Pull on the gloves—that ice and salt are cold!—and shake the bag for at least five minutes. Make sure the ice is around the cream mixture.

WHAT'S GOING ON?

The ice cools the ice cream by absorbing energy from it. (The ice also absorbs energy from you, which is why you need to wear gloves to keep warm!) Without the salt on the ice, the ice would melt when it absorbs that energy. But salt lowers the temperature at which ice melts. It makes the ice colder and better able to freeze your ice cream.

Magic Marshmallows

See what happens when you microwave marshmallows.

WHAT YOU'LL NEED:

- Large marshmallows
- A microwave-safe plate
- An adult's permission to use a microwave oven
- Oven mitts

1. Place two marshmallows on the plate. Put the plate in the microwave.

2. Set the microwave timer for one minute on **HIGH**. Watch as your marshmallows expand.

3. When the minute is over, put on the oven mitts and carefully take the plate out of the microwave.

4. Let the marshmallows cool for a few seconds, then pull one apart. Examine it, then eat it.

5. Watch the other marshmallow as it shrinks. Then form it into whatever shape you like. (You can eat this marshmallow, too.)

WHAT'S GOING ON?

After twenty seconds, your marshmallows start to puff up until they are four times their original size. That's because marshmallows are made of sugar and water wrapped around lots and lots of air bubbles. When you microwave marshmallows, the water heats up, which heats up the sugar and the air.

The air expands, and since the sugar walls of the marshmallow are also warm, they're flexible and the marshmallow puffs up. When the marshmallow cools, the bubbles of air shrink and the sugar hardens.

If you like, before you microwave the marshmallow, use food coloring and a toothpick to draw a face or whatever you like on it. Watch it expand as the marshmallow puffs up.

You can also microwave marshmallow chicks and bunnies.

DO NOT microwave your marshmallows for more than two minutes. They will turn into a black, sticky mess, and will really stink.

Bits and Bites

Ancient Egyptians made a sweet treat out of honey and the root of the marshmallow plant. Today, marshmallows are made with sugar and gelatin.

Chapter Seven

Would You Eat Tarantula?

Whether you grow up in Tennessee, Taiwan, or Cambodia, you want to know, "What's for dinner?" But while fried chicken feet might tempt you in Africa, in the United States you'd probably prefer chicken wings. And if you called Cambodia home, you might crave tarantula instead.

People eat what grows in their climate, is popular in their culture and religion, and is easily accessible. Food that's considered gross or bizarre in one place may be considered scrumptious and normal in another. Many people around the world eat insects for example, which are nutritious and, some say, delicious. But to most North Americans and Europeans, eating bugs is weird.

Despite some differences, it's astonishing how many foods, like dumplings, stews, pancakes, and noodles, are similar in countries thousands of miles apart. Great minds think alike? Yes, and food travels. Explorers, tourists, and immigrants spread food and recipes around the world.

In Africa: A Tasty Dish of . . .

Food in Africa is as diverse as the continent.

• We're all supposed to chew our food before swallowing. Right? Usually. But in Nigeria, there's one food called *foo-foo* (sometimes spelled fou-fou or fu-fu) that's gulped down without chewing. Foo-foo is a thick paste made of cornmeal and a root vegetable, like cassava or yams, that have been mashed up and boiled with water. You snip off a piece with your fingers, dip it into soup or stew, and pop it into your mouth without chewing. Foo-foo is only eaten with the right hand. (The left hand is used for less-hygienic purposes.)

• If you're invited to a traditional Ethiopian wedding, be prepared to eat a dish of fresh, raw, sliced beef accompanied by *berbere*, a fiery, spicy, peppery paste. And don't expect it to be served on a plate or handed a fork and knife. Ethiopians use an *injera*, a thick, spongy pancake, to wrap and eat their food instead.

• In South Africa, *biltong*, strips of animal buttocks, is a popular dish. Once prepared by migrant tribesmen, biltong was stored under a saddle so that the salt in the horse's sweat and the air would preserve it. Horse sweat not your cup of tea? Don't worry. These days, this chewy food is covered in salt for over an hour, dipped in vinegar, sprinkled with pepper and coriander, and then dried.

• Goat droppings, nuts, and oil—a strange combination? Not in Morocco, a country at the northern tip of the continent. Goats are attracted to the fruit of the local argan tree. Local women gather the goat's droppings and extract the strong, nutty-flavored oil. They say it's delicious in an almond-honey dessert called *amlou*.

In Australia: From Grubs to Barbie

• Curious what a grub tastes like? You can find one of these thick, wormlike insect larvae in your yard, or just head instead for Australia. The Aboriginal people in Australia are fond of grubs, especially green grubs. Children and women dig them up. Then the grubs are munched raw or rolled in ashes. They're reported to taste like almonds.

• What makes the Aboriginal people of New South Wales rejoice? The flight of the Bogon moth between November and January. When the moths fly in, the locals love to eat them.

Bits and Bites

Want to invite six friends for dinner and use only one egg? Find a giant ostrich egg and cook it. That's what they do in Central Africa.

• If you want to taste kangaroo in Australia, you'll have to go to South Australia, Tasmania, or the northern territories. By Australian law, those are the only places where kangaroo can be served.

In Europe: Delicious and Dangerous

Italy: *Never Put Pineapples on Pizza*

Do you love deep-dish pan pizza or pizza with pineapples? If you do, you are not, according to The Association of True Neapolitan Pizza, eating an authentic pizza. Authentic pizza dough must be made by hand and baked on the surface of a wood-burning oven. And don't forget to only use fresh mozzarella cheese and extra virgin olive oil. Absolutely no pineapples allowed!

Bits and Bites

Today many Australians are wild for "barbie," their word for barbeque. As for dessert, they adore a Pavlova, a treat named after a Russian ballerina. (See page 45 for more on Pavlova.)

Switzerland: *The Pharmacist Knows Everything—About Mushrooms*

The Swiss are so fond of foraging in the woods for fungi (mushrooms) that some people have accidentally eaten poison ones. To help prevent death by mushrooms, some pharmacists in Switzerland are certified to identify the good fungi from the poisonous ones.

Eastern Europe: *Ha Ha P'tcha*

Some people smile when they see wobbly food, others rush to the nearest exit. *P'tcha*, a classic Eastern European dish that's made from jellied calves' feet and garlic, makes some people smile and others gag.

The United Kingdom: *Hold On to Your Stomach*

Folks in the United Kingdom don't like wasting anything, especially food. Traditionally they used all parts of an animal in cooking. Take haggis. It's a popular Scottish dish made from the liver, heart, and lungs of a sheep, mixed with oats

France: *Not Always Frogs*

Who eats the most frogs today? The French? No! Asians eat more frogs than the French. But whether they're nibbled in Paris or Beijing, the delicate white meat of the legs is the only edible part of a frog. If you'd like to try them, a short dip in flour and a quick fry in olive oil and crushed garlic will cook them just right. And yes, like many foods, frog legs taste like chicken.

and potatoes, and stuffed inside the sheep's stomach.

Some other colorful dishes from the United Kingdom are: jellied eel, toad-in-the hole (sausages covered in batter and roasted), bubble and squeak (leftover vegetables fried in a pan with mashed potatoes; it squeaks when it cooks), bangers and mash (mashed potatoes and sausage), black pudding (sausage made from dried pigs' blood and fat), and mushy peas.

In Asia: Strange but Scrumptious

Taste a Rat, Munch a Bug in Thailand

Yes. Some Thai eat rats. They are often killed with a slingshot, cooked over an open fire, and served on a bowl of hot chili stock with sticky rice. Some Thai also relish an assortment of bugs, such as yellow ants and chilies, maggots, grasshoppers, king scorpions, fried spiders, hornet grubs, and cockroaches. Those who've tasted these Thai treats say they're not bad at all.

How About Tarantula in Cambodia?

In the town of Skuon, not far from Phnom Penh, the capital of Cambodia, the eight-legged tarantula has become a popular food. The practice began in the war years of the Khmer Rouge (1975–1979) when food was scarce. To the local's surprise, they liked this eight-legged dish and have continued to nibble on it till today.

Eating Rover

In many parts of the Philippines and Korea, some breeds of dogs were not considered pets, but dinner. In Korea, eating dogs goes back thousands of years. Just check out wall paintings from the fourth century CE. That tradition has been changing in recent years, and there are now ordinances in both countries against eating dogs.

Yakkity-Yak in Tibet

In Tibet, it's all about the yak, a large, hairy ox. What does yak meat taste like? Ask a Golok, a nomadic Tibetan who eats dried yak meat on his trek up a mountain. Tibetans also savor a cool sip of female yak milk called *dzi*. They make butter, cheese, and yogurt out of the yak milk. Then they take the yak butter, ferment it, and stir it into tea. Yak butter is so versatile that sometimes the Goloks smear it on their skin to protect against the cold, dry air.

Durian: *King of Fruit or King of Stink?*

Not everybody agrees that the durian deserves the title "king of fruit," but some swear it tastes sublime.

That is if you can get over the odor. People have compared the smell of a durian to that of rotting sewage. It's so strong that the fruit is banned in many public places in Malaysia. After eating it, your breath may reek for as long as six hours.

In Latin America: Hot, Raw, or Crunchy?

• Want to burn your mouth? Have a habanera pepper. They're the hottest peppers known to man and are grown in Mexico and the Yucatan Peninsula. (Find out more about hot peppers on page 100).

• How about a really different lollipop? The Mexican tequila sucker would fit that bill. Its ingredients include high-fructose corn syrup and insect larvae.

• If you go to the movies in Colombia, you might bring along roasted ants, a crunchy treat with a bit of a smoky flavor served in paper cups. Then again, you might not.

• And then there's the iguana. In Honduras, Belize, Panama, and the Yucatan Peninsula of Mexico, you might find one wandering around your house. Catch it and try one of the many iguana recipes. Some cookbooks suggest you can even turn it into tacos.

In North America: Not Just Hamburger and Fries

• In North America, we think we eat "normal" food like bread with peanut butter and jelly, but to some in Australia and New Zealand, the idea of that sandwich makes them groan. The jelly, in particular, is a total turnoff.

• So what would they think of some of North America's more exotic foods, like Texas rattlesnake? Every year in March in Sweetwater, Texas, the locals host an annual Rattlesnake Roundup (the world's largest), and hundreds of snakes are cooked and served.

• How about alligator on a stick? It's battered, deep-fried, and has a chewy taste. Some people say that the key to cooking alligator is to wash the alligator well and cook it like you would fried chicken or ribs. And the place to eat it? Come down to Louisiana for alligator treats.

• Head for Hawaii for the unique and, some say, nasty taste of *poi*. Poi is mashed taro root, and for many Hawaiians it's the first food they had as infants. But for those who have not developed a taste for poi, it's been compared to eating wallpaper paste.

Chapter Eight

Largest, Longest, Tallest, Stinkiest

When some people see a custard pie, they can't wait to dig in with their forks. Other people just itch to throw it at someone. During the biggest custard pie fight ever—held in London, England—3,312 pies were thrown in just three minutes by only twenty people. No one knows how long it took to clean up afterward.

That's just one of the incredible food records you'll read about in this chapter. Get ready to read about the deadliest food, the sweetest food, the most expensive food, and much more.

You Ate How Much?

• How many hot dogs could you eat in twelve minutes? Think you could beat the record of 66? Or if you like cheesecake, could you choke down more than 11 pounds (5 kilograms) in nine minutes?

Food-eating contests are more popular in the United States than in any other county. Competitive eaters, sometimes called gurgitators, take their sport very seriously. The International Federation of Competitive Eating referees all matches and hands out more than $230,000 in prize money each year.

You might think that all competitive eaters are large males. Actually, the person who holds the records for eating the most lobster meat, hard-boiled eggs, pork and beans, and much more is a woman who weighs just 105 pounds (48 kilograms)!

As you can imagine, all that eating isn't good for the human body. Stretching the stomach again and again may keep it from working properly. Also, competitors have died from choking during a contest. Many people dislike the contests since they encourage overeating when so many people in the world are hungry.

Bits and Bites

Here's one record that probably won't be smashed for some time: In 2001, a man in England ate thirty-six hissing Madagascar cockroaches in one minute.

World's Biggest Sweet Tooth

• There are some big candy lovers out there. The world's largest piece of candy was made in Diemen, Netherlands, in May 1990. This chocolate almond sweet weighed 4,078½ pounds (1,850 kilograms).

• Don't budge if you like fudge! The biggest slab of fudge ever was cooked, stirred, and poured on

Bits and Bites

The Swiss hold the record for eating the most chocolate. Each year, the average person in Switzerland eats 230 chocolate bars.

November 5, 2004, in Toronto, Canada. It weighed 3,010 pounds (1,365 kilograms)—that's as much as a car!

• Chocolate often inspires people to make record-shattering treats. In November 2002, the largest box of chocolates ever created was on display in Chicago. It weighed 3,226 pounds (1,463 kilograms) and contained 90,090 chocolates.

• The biggest chocolate bar ever was made in Turin, Italy, in 2000 and weighed 5,026 pounds (2,280 kilograms), or about as much as a small elephant. It was big enough to treat you and about 23,000 of your closest friends to a regular-size chocolate bar each.

Sour Puss and Sweetie Pie

• The bitterest substance on Earth is denatonium benzoate, a chemical created by scientists. Why would anyone want to make a bitter taste? Bitrex, as the chemical is also known, is added to poisonous liquids so people—especially young children who can't read the warning labels—and pets won't drink them.

Bathroom cleaner, rat poison, and antifreeze all usually have a dollop of Bitrex in them.

• Artificial sweeteners, such as NutraSweet or Equal, are two hundred to three hundred times sweeter than regular sugar. But there are other chemicals, known as bernardame and sucrononate that are more than 200,000 times sweeter than sugar. Don't go looking in the grocery story for these last two—they're used only in the lab, not in food.

Yuck, Yuck, Yuck!

• Tripe (the lining of a cow's stomach), snails, oysters, kidneys—those are some of the foods that people hate most. You might think that everyone's different when it comes to meals they love or loathe, but actually most people are fairly similar.

For one thing, we tend to avoid bitter tastes. That's actually a good survival mechanism because it makes us stay away from poisonous foods. We're also designed to like sweet foods, as well as fatty ones, because they're good sources of energy in times when it's tough to find anything to eat.

Turning up our noses at foods that are slimy or rubbery (like tripe) keeps us from eating food that's gone bad. And for some reason, people don't like food made from slithery or even ugly animals! If you have a bad memory of a time when you were served a certain dish, it will probably be a long time before that meal finds its way to your list of favorites.

Most Dangerous Food

• Care to guess what's the deadliest dish out there? Poison mushrooms? Moldy cheese? Broccoli? Would you imagine that the riskiest food is a fish? *Fugu*, also known as the puffer fish or blowfish, contains deadly poison in its organs. Despite this, it's considered a great delicacy in Japan.

Chefs work for seven years before they receive a license to prepare fugu. No wonder they have to study so hard—eating just a tiny drop of the toxin in fugu can paralyze and kill you. And it takes only a small slip of the knife while fugu is being prepared for the toxins to get into the part you're going to eat.

Experts estimate that the poison in just one fugu could kill more than thirty people. The greatest cause of food poisoning in Japan is badly prepared fugu. Each year, dozens of people die from eating fugu toxins.

How do most people describe the taste of this fish for which they risk their lives? Believe it or not, they say it has a bland flavor. Go figure.

World's Biggest Burger

• The record for the most humungous hamburger was set in February 2007 in Clearfield, Pennsylvania. The award-winning meal featured 80 pounds (36.3 kilograms) of beef. Of course the 30-pound (13.6 kilograms) bun had to be specially made to match the powerful patty.

Then the toppings were added. They included 160 slices of cheese, 12 tomatoes, 5 onions, and 1 pound (.45 kilograms) each of ketchup, lettuce, mayo, mustard, and relish. And don't forget the pickles and banana peppers.

The final result weighed 123 pounds (55.8 kilograms). And how big across is this champion cheeseburger? It's as large as you and your friend standing side by side. Think you could eat one? The price will set you back $379.

What's That Smell?

• When even people who like a food agree that it smells like sewage or a garbage dump, then you know you can stop searching for the world's stinkiest food. Stinky tofu is made by marinating tofu in a liquid made from rotten vegetables. When the tofu is stinky, it's fried and served. Fans say the smellier it is, the better it tastes. Stinky tofu is especially popular in East and Southeast Asia.

Bits and Bites

If you prefer French cheese, try Vieux Boulogne. It's so smelly that you can't carry it on public transit in France.

• Or maybe you'd rather end your meal with cheese. If you're a fan of the animated characters Wallace & Gromit, then you already know about Stinking Bishop. This British cheese gets its name from the pear of the same name. As the cheese matures, it's washed in Stinking Bishop pear cider. If you like a cheese that tastes like dirty socks, then this is for you.

Bits and Bites

The largest restaurant in the world is the Royal Dragon Restaurant in Bangkok. It can seat about five thousand customers. There are more than one thousand dishes on the menu and servers zip around on roller skates.

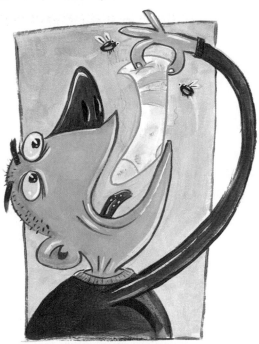

Biggest Breakfasts

• Some people wake up with a big appetite. The largest breakfast ever was served in Taiwan in 2001.

About 23,291 people were fed and the menu included 1,247 gallons (4,720 liters) of milk and 4,232 pounds (1,920 kilograms) of bread. That's more than 2,800 loaves of bread and enough milk to fill at least forty bathtubs!

• The world's largest omelet was made with 160,000 eggs and had an area of 1,383 square feet

(128.5 square meters), or about the size of a large apartment. People gulped it down in Japan in 1994. Want some sausage to go with that omelet? The record for the longest sausage is 37 miles (59.14 kilometers).

• San Antonio, Texas, was the scene of the World's Largest Pancake Breakfast in 2001. If you stacked up all the pancakes served, they'd tower more than 2 miles (3 kilometers) high!

• Ready for lunch? Maybe you've got room for a bite of the world's largest sandwich ever. This corned beef biggie was made in Roseville, Michigan, in 2005 and weighed 5,440 pounds (2,467.5 kilograms).

You've Got What in That Cup?

• Some gourmet foods sound so weird that it's hard to imagine anyone would actually eat them. Take the world's rarest coffee, known as Kopi Luwak, for example.

This coffee comes from Indonesia, where a wild cat known as a luwak lives. The cat eats ripe coffee berries. Its body breaks down the outer fruit, but the beans pass right through its digestive system and out the other end. The beans are left in the cat's dung heaps, where they're harvested by workers. Then the beans are cleaned and roasted, and finally sold for about $500 per 1 pound (454 grams) bag!

Fans of this rare coffee say the luwak's stomach acids give the coffee a unique taste that's described as—big surprise—earthy and musty.

Tree-mendous Record

• Jay Gwaltney was well aware that he'd have to do something pretty incredible to win the "What's the Most Outrageous Thing You Would Do?" contest in 1980. He knew he'd have to beat out six thousand competitors for the $10,000 prize. So the nineteen-year-old university student decided to eat a tree.

Dressed in a tuxedo and seated at a table elegantly set with fine china and candles, Jay got to work on his 11-foot- (3.4-meter-) high dinner. His cutlery? A pair of pruning shears.

Jay ate the birch tree branch by branch, all the way from the top-most leafy twigs to the tip of the roots. A little French salad dressing helped wash it all down. Still, eating the tree took Jay eighteen hours, spread out over three days.

Oddly enough, when Jay was finished, he complained of having an upset stomach. However, he later said, "As far as trees go, it's not bad." By the way, Jay won the contest and the $10,000.

Heavy Metal

• Michel Lotito is better known as Monsieur Mangetout, which translates from French as "Mister Eat-Anything." Consuming weird items is how Michel makes his living. He's been eating metal, glass, and more for about fifty years. Michel munches on approximately 2 pounds (908 grams) of metal each day. Talk about getting enough iron in your diet!

Bicycles, televisions, supermarket carts—they're all on Monsieur Mangetout's menu. Before every eating performance, he drinks mineral oil and gulps down lots of water during his meal. Then he takes apart the appliance or vehicle, cuts up the pieces and chows down. When Michel ate an airplane, it took him about two years before the last bolt disappeared down his gullet.

Although Monsieur Mangetout has been eating his strange diet since he was nine, don't try it yourself. Doctors have found that Michel has a unique stomach. Its lining is twice as thick as a normal stomach lining. And the acids in his stomach are unusually powerful.

Chapter Nine

Who Invented That?

Imagine a world without Jell-O, ketchup, peanut butter, frozen food, the can opener, or restaurants. These foods, products, and places didn't always exist, but now they're part of our lives. Some were created by accident, others to win a prize, but most were invented because someone had a great idea.

jars, then sealed and heated them to remove the air. In 1810, he won Napoleon's prize, but his glass jars were heavy and broke easily.

The same year, an English merchant, Peter Durand, invented a tin-plated iron can. Soon Englishmen John Hall and Bryan Donkin manufactured tin cans. But their cans were heavy and clumsy, and it was impossible to get food out of them without a hammer and chisel.

Can It!

• Emperor Napoleon of France had a problem. In 1795, it took such a long time to transport food to the battlefront, it often went bad before it reached the soldiers. Napoleon didn't want his men to starve, so he offered a prize to anyone who could come up with a way to preserve food.

A shopkeeper named Nicholas Appert was convinced he had the solution. He noticed that if food was kept away from air, it didn't spoil quickly. Appert packed food in glass

In 1858, Ezra Warner of Waterbury, Connecticut, invented and patented the first can opener. Finally you could open your can and eat your beans or tomatoes without digging into the toolbox.

Cool Food

• Hungry? Just open your refrigerator and pull out a snack. But once, there were no refrigerators, freezers, or frozen food.

• There was ice, of course. The Chinese stored ice in icehouses as far back as 1,000 BCE to keep food cold. Icehouses were still being used in Europe in the nineteenth century, but they didn't work well if it was hot outside or you lived in a warm climate.

Jacob Perkins, an American living in London, invented a machine that produced ice in 1834. But ice-making machines only made ice. They didn't store food. And after the warm winters of 1889 and 1890, severe natural ice shortages encouraged people to come up with something better—a mechanical refrigerator.

People could now keep food cold for longer and freeze it, too. But when they defrosted their food, ice crystals formed and food tasted mushy.

In the early 1900s, a man named Clarence Birdseye visited Labrador, Canada, and noticed that the natives quickly froze fish right after catching them. When the fish defrosted, they tasted as fresh as if they'd just been hauled out of the sea. Birdseye started fast-freezing small batches of food, and a whole new frozen food industry developed.

Sandwich, Anyone?

• Most people think that the Earl of Sandwich was the inventor of the sandwich. After all, his name's on it. Not so. The famous Jewish rabbi Hillel the Elder, who lived in the first century BCE, made the first recorded sandwich. But his sandwich used matzoh, unleavened bread, instead of bread.

People continued to eat meat with bread in some form throughout the sixteenth and seventeenth centuries, but the Earl of Sandwich made this everyday food popular. The earl, a well-known gambler, hated to stop gambling even while eating. One day he ordered his valet to bring him his favorite meat, salt beef, tucked between two slices of bread so he would have one hand free to gamble. People liked the earl's idea so much, they were soon clamoring to eat the "same as Sandwich."

How French Is French Toast?

• Some version of French toast (bread dipped into eggs and milk and then fried) has been made around the world since ancient Roman times. The French call their dish *pain perdu* (lost bread), while in England, it's been called eggy bread and sometimes spread with marmite (a sticky, brown paste made from yeast extract) before frying. In Australia, it's often served with tomato sauce. In Italy, cheese is sandwiched between two pieces of bread and then dipped in egg and fried.

What's Bread Without Peanut Butter?

• Peanut butter has been around for centuries. Peanuts were munched on as early as 950 BCE. The ancient Incas made a pastelike substance from it. Peanuts then traveled from South America to Africa via the early explorers, and the Spaniards introduced it to North Americans. Virginians began growing peanuts in the mid-1840s.

The Three Spreadable M's— Margarine, Mayonnaise, and Miracle Whip

Margarine: The food we call margarine refers to a variety of spreadable edibles that substitute for butter. The name originated with the discovery of "margaric acid" by Michel Eugene Chevreul in 1813. In 1869, Emperor Louis Napoleon III of France offered a prize to anyone who could make a butter substitute for the armed forces and the lower classes. A French chemist named Hippolyte Mege-Mouries used Chevreul's acid and invented a substance called oleomargarine, later called margarine.

Mayonnaise: There are lots of stories about the origin of this blend of egg yolks and oil, flavored with vinegar, mustard, herbs, and spices. An often-told tale is that when the French Duke Richelieu captured Port Mayon on the Spanish island of Minorca in 1756, the duke's chef was forced to substitute olive oil for cream in a sauce. Delighted with the results, the chef called his new creation mayonnaise in honor of Port Mayon.

Miracle Whip: Are you a fan of Miracle Whip? This substitute for mayonnaise is made of water, soybean oil, vinegar, fructose, egg yolks, salt, mustard, and flour. Advertised as having half the fat of mayonnaise, it was invented at Max Crosset's Café in Illinois. Crosset had no idea how successful his product would become. He sold it to the Kraft food company in 1931 for the paltry sum of $300.

Jell-O: A Wiggly Delight

• Jell-O began in 1845 when Peter Cooper, a famous inventor, patented a product set with gelatin. No one wanted it.

• In 1897, Pearle Wait, a carpenter in Leroy, New York, added fruit flavors to gelatin and stuck the dry mixture into a box. His wife, May, called their new product Jell-O, but the Waits couldn't sell it, either.

• In 1899, Wait sold Jell-O to a fellow townsman, Frank Woodward, for only $450. But the public wouldn't go for Jell-O no matter how hard he tried.

• Woodward was about to give up when suddenly their advertising paid off. By 1904, when the company introduced the Jell-O girl, the gelatin was firmly established. And by 1934, when comedian Jack Benny plugged it along with a snappy jingle that sang out the letters of Jell-O, its popularity soared.

The Big Three: Hamburgers, French Fries, and Ketchup

Hamburger—*Once Upon a Time on a Horse*

• In the twelfth century, on the way to conquering China, the fierce Mongol emperor Genghis Khan and his horsemen had little time to stop and cook. In their rush, they decided to form patties out of lamb or mutton bits and place them under their saddles to soften the meat as they rode into battle. When it was time to eat, all they had to do was pull out their tenderized patty and munch it raw.

When Genghis Khan's grandson, Kublai Khan (1215–1294), invaded Moscow, he brought the raw beef dish along. The Russians didn't enjoy being vanquished by the Mongols, or Tartars as they were also called, but they liked the new meat dish they named steak tartare.

A few centuries later, the Germans in Hamburg traded with the Russians and discovered steak tartare. They called it hamburger, after their city, and they liked it both raw and grilled. Their hamburger contained salted and smoked minced beef, mixed with onions and breadcrumbs. When the Germans immigrated to the United States in the 1850s, they brought along the hamburger.

French Fries—*French?*

• It's not clear how and where the French fry was born, but many people believe a French chef created it. As evidence they point to a note American president Jefferson made in 1801. He wrote that he'd eaten "potatoes deep fried while raw in small slices." There are even recipes in French cookbooks for French fries that date back to the mid-1700s.

Ketchup— *Pickled Fish?*

• Who would have thought that ketchup began as a pickled fish sauce called *ketsiap*? The Chinese

used ke-tsiap, as did the Malaysians and Indonesians.

• Ketchup as we know it probably started in the United States, when Americans acquired a taste for tomatoes. In 1801, a recipe for tomato-based ketchup was published in the American cookbook *The Sugar House Book*.

• Tomatoes are now popular all over North America and Europe. In Spain, they are so passionate about the tomato, they've been holding a Tomatina festival since the 1940s in Valencia. During the festival, more than thirty thousand people pelt one another and the city with tomatoes.

Is Pasta a Noodle, or Is a Noodle Pasta?

• According to some people, there's a big difference between the two. Noodles are made from wheat flour while pasta is usually made from durum flour. But to many people, they are both part of the same food family.

• Conquering Arabs introduced pasta to Sicily in the twelfth century. Sicily is now part of Italy, the country most people associate with pasta today. The Italians have embraced pasta and created wonderful shapes and sauces that are loved around the world.

Bits and Bites

In the 1700s in Naples, pasta was made by hand. The pasta maker sat on a support while kneading the dough with his feet. In the early 1800s, the king of Naples, Ferdinand the II, was disgusted by the idea of eating pasta kneaded by someone's stinky feet. King Ferdinand hired an engineer to invent a machine and create a more hygienic food.

Around the World with Tea

• An ancient tale says that tea was the bright idea of Chinese emperor Shen Nung, who insisted all water was boiled so it would be clean of contaminants and drinkable. One day while traveling, his servants, as usual, boiled water. This time dried leaves from a bush fell into the water, creating a brownish liquid. Instead of dumping the whole thing, the emperor tasted it and proclaimed the mixture refreshing. A new drink was created.

• In the mid-1500s, a Portuguese priest tasted and liked it and started shipping it to Lisbon. From there, the Dutch, French, and Baltic countries picked it up. It became quite the rage in Holland. Dutchman Peter Stuyvesant brought it to New Amsterdam (now New York) in the New World in 1650 and the locals loved it. England began a love affair with tea from 1650 on, and they've never stopped sipping it (although coffee is now giving tea real competition).

Bits and Bites

In 1908, New York tea merchant Thomas Sullivan sent samples of tea to his customers in small, elegant silk bags. Some of his customers thought that the bags were supposed to be dipped in boiling water to make tea. When Sullivan heard about their mistake, he realized he'd accidentally invented a new product. Sullivan used gauze sachets instead of the fine silk bags, and in 1920, began production of the first commercial tea bags.

Restaurants—For Suffering Stomachs

• There have always been places serving food and drink to the public. Inns date back to the beginning of trade. In Roman days, you could purchase roasted meats and poultry in cook shops. There were take-out places in the Middle Ages where you could pick up a pie or a pastry. English taverns and beefsteak houses were early forms of restaurants where people met friends and dined.

But the restaurant as we know it today (a place where there's a selection of food to order from a menu) was opened in Paris by a soup vendor named Boulanger in 1765. A form of the word *restaurant* appeared on his door in this way: *Vente ad me omnes qui stomacho laboratis et ego restaurabo.* That means "Come all ye whose stomachs suffer and I will restore you." Boulanger served a variety of soups, fowl, and fresh eggs on bare marble-topped tables. He was soon copied.

True or False

1. The residents of Russia eat out at restaurants more than any other people. _____

2. The most popular day to eat out in the United States is Friday. _____

3. Americans eat almost 35 percent of their meals away from home. _____

4. Salmon and shrimp are the most popular seafoods in American restaurants. _____

5. Seattle is home to the first revolving restaurant. _____

The answers are on page 112.

Chapter Ten

Everything but the Kitchen Sink

Get ready to read an amazing collection of food trivia. Where does the expression "everything but the kitchen sink" come from? No one knows for sure, but most people think it started in the 1940s during World War II. To help fight the war, people at home contributed all they could, especially metal for tanks, bullets, and more. About the only thing that couldn't be used were porcelain kitchen sinks. Everything but the kitchen sink has come to mean "just about anything."

How Many Elephants?

• You spend more than fifteen full days every year doing nothing but eating. Can you believe it? Does your jaw hurt from just thinking about all of that chewing?

How much are you eating during that half a month? Every year, you gulp down about 170 grocery bags of food. Try carrying all of those sacks home from the grocery store! Phew! Think that's heavy? Over your whole life, you'll eat approximately 60,000 to 100,000 pounds (27,200 to 45,359 kilograms) of food. That's about the same weight of food as six to ten elephants!

And don't forget you need more than food to survive. You've also got to swallow a lot of water. In a year, you should drink about 3,000 cups (710 liters).

Hot, Hot, Hot!

• Yeow! You've just bitten into what you thought was a mild chili pepper only to find your mouth is on fire. What's causing you so much pain is the chemical capsaicin. It has no taste or smell, but it works directly on the pain receptors in your mouth and throat.

Bits and Bites

Approximately 66 million people in the United States suffer from food poisoning every year. About five thousand become so ill that they die from it.

hot stuff. Water doesn't really help: Since capsaicin is an oil, it doesn't mix with the water. Instead, water just spreads the pain around your mouth.

• Scientists have a scale for measuring a pepper's heat. Bell peppers—the ones that are green, red, orange, or yellow and are often raw in salads—rate zero on the scale. The hottest pepper, a red savina habanero, scores a fiery 577,000. Pure capsaicin is almost off the scale at sixteen million! In a pepper, the capsaicin is mostly found in the white ribs and seeds.

• Next time you find your mouth is hotter than hot from eating peppers, what's the best remedy? Some people say you should drink milk or eat rice or bread—they all absorb the capsaicin. Another option is to drink tomato juice or eat a slice of lemon or lime to counteract the

Nuts to You

• Cashew nuts grow on large trees, at the tip of a pea-shaped fruit called a cashew apple. The apple is safe and can be eaten raw, but the nut can't. It's surrounded by a shell that contains a poisonous oil. That's why you'll never find cashew nuts in the shell at a grocery store.

• To make cashew nuts edible,

they're roasted. But stand back! Even the smoke from cashews is poisonous. Next, the brittle, baked shells are broken away. This has to be done by hand since the odd shape of the nuts and their fragility make cashews impossible to shell by machine. Skilled workers carefully use hammers to crack the shells. Then the nuts are baked for twelve hours to remove any remaining poison. A spotted skin is peeled off and the cashews are ready to be eaten.

Doesn't it make you wonder how anyone ever discovered how delicious cashews are?

Death by Molasses

• January 15, 1919, was a sunny day in the north end of Boston. Shortly after noon, the temperature was a balmy—for the middle of winter—43°F (6°C). Many of the workers in the area were outside happily enjoying their lunch break.

Suddenly there was a low, deep rumble. The ground shook. People looked up in horror as a huge tank of molasses split open. Chunks of metal from the tank flew everywhere, piercing bystanders and buildings for blocks. With a roar, more than 2.3 million gallons (8.7 million liters) of molasses burst from the tank. An 8-foot (2.4-meter) wave of thick goo surged forward, crushing everything in its path.

The molasses flowed into a nearby storage building. Clerks inside desperately fought the yellow-brown torrent but were sucked down to their deaths. The floors groaned under the weight of the molasses and finally gave way, killing the workers in the basement.

The sticky wall of death swept on, moving too fast for people to outrun it. Panic-stricken horses became trapped in the molasses and had to be shot and put out of their misery. Rescuers suddenly found themselves caught in the gloopy muck as it sucked off their boots.

What made the tank burst? People still don't know for sure. Weather reports show that a few days before the flood, the temperature in the area was just 2°F (17°C). The incredible rise in temperature in such a short time may have caused the molasses to expand and break the tank. Others believe the tank had never been strong enough to hold so much molasses, and it was just a matter of time before such a calamity occurred.

By the time the destruction was over, 21 people were dead and 150 were injured. The neighborhood was devastated. It took a long time to clean up the mess of this horrible accident. Months after the flood, people continued to stick to the goo as they walked through the devastated area.

One Calorie, Two Calories . . .

• A calorie is a way of measuring the amount of energy available in the food you digest.

• No matter what you do, you use up calories. Even when you're sleeping, you burn half a calorie each minute, or about a scoop of vanilla ice cream each night. For every minute that you sit reading this book, you're using up one calorie. The next time your parents catch you staying up late reading in bed, just tell them you're trying to burn more calories! Then turn out the light.

• Whenever you eat something, your digestive system breaks it down into molecules that it can shoot through your bloodstream. The food

molecules end up in the cells of your body, where they're either absorbed and used right away or stored. When you eat more calories than you burn, your body stores the extra energy and you put on weight.

It's Easy Being Green

• Crunchy, crisp, and tart—around the world, Granny Smith apples are favorites. But is this green fruit named after a real person?

Maria Ann Sherwood was born in England in 1799. When she was nineteen, she married Thomas Smith, and in 1838 they sailed to Australia. The Smiths lived in an area near Sydney where fruit trees flourished. By the time Maria was in her late sixties, or old enough to be a granny, she'd grown an apple tree with beautiful green apples. They were great for cooking and eating, and stored well, too. By 1896, Granny Smith's apples were being shipped across the globe.

It's All in the Numbers

• Did you know that the amount of pizza that Americans eat every day would cover about ninety football fields? That's an average of 350 slices per second. Each year, people in the United States eat approximately three billion pizzas— about forty-six slices have your name on them! You could eat those slices in any one of the more than 61,000 pizzerias across the country.

• When it comes to varieties, rice has pizza beat by a long shot. There are more than 15,000 types. With names like Forbidden, Baldo, Popcorn, and Koshihikari, it's hard to choose just one. If you want to add some color to your meal, try white, brown, black, red, or golden rice.

• Every American eats about 20 pounds (9 kilograms) of rice each year. The biggest rice lovers are the people of the United Arab Emirates, who eat more than 450 pounds (204 kilograms) per year!

Hash House Greek

Long before there were fast-food restaurants, there were diners, or hash houses. The waiters and waitresses who worked there came up with their own secret language to make their work more interesting. They called their code Hash House Greek. For instance, "bossy in a bowl" was the servers' special phrase for beef stew, because bossy was once a common name for a cow. "Adam and Eve on a raft" meant two poached eggs on toast.

Can you speak Hash House Greek? Try matching the expressions below with the foods they describe. The answers are on page 112.

1. Cackleberries   a) Milk

2. Cowboy with spurs   b) Pepper

3. Houseboat   c) Olive

4. Moo juice   d) Hot dog with ketchup

5. Nervous pudding   e) Eggs

6. Fly pie   f) Banana split

7. Sneeze   g) Raisin pie

8. Wart   h) Mustard

9. Yellow paint   i) Western omelet with French fries

10. Paint a bow-wow red   j) Jell-O

Bits and Bites

During your lifetime, you'll eat about 1,400 chickens, 21 cows, 14 sheep, and 12 pigs.

Titanic Meal

It was the largest passenger steamship in the world. The *Titanic* was one of the most luxurious ships ever, and everyone believed it unsinkable. Part of its luxury was elegant, delicious, and huge meals. For what was to be a seven-day voyage, the *Titanic* carried 1,221 quarts (1,155 liters) of oysters, 800 bundles of asparagus, 5 tons (5 tonnes) of sugar, and much more.

The *Titanic* left England for its first journey across the Atlantic Ocean on Wednesday, April 10, 1912. The first-class passengers were treated to the voyage's finest dinner four days later. The eleven courses included:

1. Oysters and a selection of hors d'oeuvres
2. Cream of barley soup or consommé
3. Poached salmon
4. Filet mignon, chicken, or vegetable marrow (a type of squash, like zucchini)
5. Lamb, duckling, or beef, with potatoes, peas, carrots, and rice
6. Sorbet or punch
7. Squab (fledgling pigeon)
8. Asparagus salad
9. Pâté
10. Fruit pudding, peaches in jelly, éclairs with ice cream
11. Fresh fruit and cheese

That fantastic meal was the last served on the *Titanic*. A few hours later, the mighty ship hit an iceberg and the unthinkable happened: The *Titanic* began to sink. Bakers were already hard at work preparing bread and rolls for the next day's meals. As passengers jumped into lifeboats, the bakers made sure bread went with them. Of the 2,223 passengers and crew aboard the *Titanic*, only 706 survived the horrible disaster.

Space Food

• Wherever people have gone, food has gone with them, even into the cold, black depths of space. Space station crew members eat three meals a day, plus a snack, and they usually lose weight. Each meal costs about $100, mostly because of its packaging as well as the testing that's gone into preparing it.

The five foods that astronauts request most are (in order): shrimp cocktail, lemonade, steak, M&M's, and brownies. What would you pick if you were orbiting Earth?

One thing space travelers have to leave at home are sodas. Because of the low gravity, the bubbles of carbon dioxide in the drinks go through the astronauts' stomach. Here on Earth, those bubbles are burped out. Experts don't know what effect those bubbles can have, so scientists have banned them.

What else can't astronauts eat? They're told not to chow down on baked beans before a flight for obvious reasons! In fact, the National Aeronautics and Space Administration (NASA) has developed a system to determine which foods are gas-free for launch and which should stay on Earth.

Answers

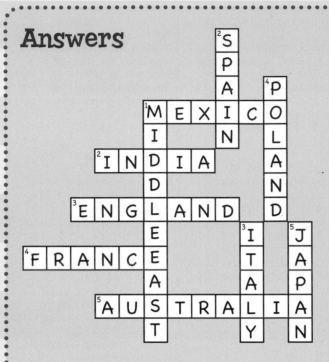

Pg. 27

ACROSS: 1. Mexico, 2. India, 3. England, 4. France, 5. Australia.

DOWN: 1. Middle East, 2. Spain, 3. Italy, 4. Poland, 5. Japan.

Pg. 35

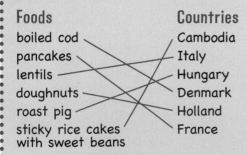

Foods
boiled cod
pancakes
lentils
doughnuts
roast pig
sticky rice cakes with sweet beans

Countries
Cambodia
Italy
Hungary
Denmark
Holland
France

Pg. 47

1. a, 2. b, 3. b, 4. b

Pg. 97

1. *False: The Russians eat out only 0.3 times per month. The people of Hong Kong eat out 8.7 meals per month.* 2. *False: Saturday* 3. *True* 4. *True* 5. *False: The Seattle Space Needle was the second revolving restaurant. La Ronde Restaurant in the Ala Moana Shopping Center in Honolulu, Hawaii, was the first. It no longer exists.*

Pg. 105

1. e, 2. i, 3. f, 4. a, 5. j, 6. g, 7. b, 8. c, 9. h, 10. d.